P9-CFG-506

EFFECTIVE PHRASES FOR PERFORMANCE APPRAISALS

A GUIDE TO SUCCESSFUL EVALUATIONS

Publishing Since 1978

NEAL PUBLICATIONS, INC.
127 West Indiana Avenue
Perrysburg, Ohio 43551-1578 U.S.A.

Publishers of

"The #1 Guide to Performance Appraisals"
Doing it right!

"Job Survival Strategies"
A guide for turbulent times

"Effective Letters for Business,
Professional and Personal Use"
A guide to successful correspondence

EFFECTIVE PHRASES FOR PERFORMANCE APPRAISALS
A Guide To Successful Evaluations

Neal Publications, Inc.
127 West Indiana Avenue — P.O. Box 451
Perrysburg, Ohio 43552-0451 U.S.A.

First Edition	1978
Two Printings	
Second Edition	1981
Three Printings	
Third Edition	1983
Eight Printings	
Fourth Edition	1986
Eight Printings	
Fifth Edition	1988
Eight Printings	
Sixth Edition	1991
Eight Printings	
Seventh Edition	1994
Eight Printings	
Eighth Edition	1997
Eight Printings	
Ninth Edition	2000
Eight Printings	
Tenth Edition	2003
Second Printing	2003
Third Printing	2003
Fourth Printing	2004
Fifth Printing	2004

Copyright 1978, 1981, 1983, 1986, 1988, 1991,
1994, 1997, 2000, 2003 by
James E. Neal, Jr.
Printed in the United States of America

ISBN 1-882423-10-0

SAN 240-8198

Library of Congress Control Number: 2002110968

FOREWORD

A major responsibility faced by every person in a managerial or supervisory position is the evaluation of employee performance. Increasingly, performance reviews are also being conducted by peers, subordinates and customers. Many individuals have also found the need to make self-evaluations.

This guide is designed to help the appraiser in selecting phrases and words that accurately describe a broad range of commonly rated factors.

The phrases contained in this handbook are extremely positive and reflect superior performance. By simply altering the phrases, it is possible to describe areas in need of improvement. For example, "Excels in delegating routine tasks to subordinates" can easily be changed to, "You can improve your effectiveness by delegating routine tasks to subordinates."

In addition, the phrases need to be substantiated with factual documentation at every opportunity. As an example, "Demonstrates sound cost effectiveness" may be expanded to "Demonstrates sound cost effectiveness as shown by your ability to achieve a 10% reduction in departmental

(continued)

expenses through the first six months compared to last year."

The same phrase may be used to describe unsatisfactory performance by stating "Since your departmental expenses are 10% over budget for the first six months compared to last year," you are expected to "Demonstrate sound cost effectiveness by meeting your year-end budget."

Phrases are continuously added and revised to describe ever changing job responsibilities in today's workplace. This expanded edition particularly reflects the growing emphasis on coaching and counseling. Additional phrases have also been added to address the popularity of project management and management vision.

While every effort has been made to avoid duplication, some headings are closely interwoven by their very nature. For example, a person using the "Supervisory Skills" section may also find the "Management Ability " section helpful.

The guide has been purchased by many thousands of users including individuals, associations, corporations, consultants, educational institutions, law enforcement agencies, libraries, hospitals, departments of the government and military personnel around the world.

CONTENTS

I. EFFECTIVE PHRASES

EFFECTIVE PHRASES

I. EFFECTIVE PHRASES

(continued)

EFFECTIVE PHRASES

ACCURACY

recognizes the importance of accuracy

holds people accountable for accuracy

performs with a high degree of accuracy

performs with consistent accuracy

achieves results with accuracy and precision

maintains high statistical accuracy

expects perfection

strives for perfection

excels in achieving perfection

avoids mistakes and errors

continuously strives to reduce errors

develops realistic tolerance levels

conforms to strict tolerances

meets precise standards

meets rigid specifications

keeps accurate records

maintains accurate documentation

(continued)

ACCURACY

provides explicit documentations

is meticulous with detail

gives meticulous attention to detail

excels in detail checking

forecasts with extreme accuracy

uses sound statistical methods to forecast with accuracy

makes accurate predictions about future trends, directions and developments

ACHIEVEMENT

achieves optimal levels of personal performance and accomplishment

consistently achieves optimal outcomes

is a solid achiever

provides strong evidence of specific accomplishments

excels in developing programs that deliver results

produces a tangible, positive impact

achieves consistent effectiveness

achieves consistently high results

excels in achieving outstanding project results

achieves bottom-line results

achieves lasting results

exceeds the norm

accomplishes more with fewer people

demonstrates the ability to achieve desired results

focuses on results

attains results without negative side effects

attains results through positive actions

ADMINISTRATION

demonstrates a high level of administrative competence

continuously examines administrative effectiveness and seeks better procedures

encourages administrative efficiency and effectiveness

achieves high administrative output

avoids burdening management with administrative details

effectively uses exception reporting to keep management informed

clearly establishes administrative rules and regulations

enumerates and specifies procedures for implementing and administering written policies

develops policies and procedures to improve department

improves administrative support systems

supplies necessary support services

provides a wide range of administrative services

develops successful administrative strategies

excels in simplifying systems and reducing paperwork

ADMINISTRATION

excels in eliminating unnecessary paperwork

avoids unnecessary correspondence

effectively controls paperwork

manages paperwork efficiently and effectively

improves administrative efficiency through the effective use of forms

displays excellent skills in organizing, filing and retrieving records

establishes effective systems for record retention

establishes effective systems for information retrieval

capably manages records retention program giving proper attention to legal, tax and operational concerns

is highly skilled in electronic records management

excels in maintaining electronic files

keeps simple records with little duplication

keeps filing systems current

maintains current records

(continued)

ADMINISTRATION

effectively handles information overload

is able to cope with the information explosion

establishes effective systems for information retrieval

understands and applies basic statistical methods

makes effective use of statistical applications

uses sound statistical control techniques

properly controls the release of proprietary information

takes appropriate measures to protect intellectual property

recognizes the importance of protecting trade secrets

capably oversees and maintains the confidentiality of vital records

respects confidential information

maintains complete confidentiality

makes effective use of office equipment

keeps abreast of new technologies to improve administrative efficiency

utilizes improved technology for administrative support

ANALYTICAL SKILLS

demonstrates a strong power of analytical reasoning

displays strong analytical qualities

demonstrates a strong ability to analyze problems

is very methodical in solving problems

utilizes a variety of analytical techniques to solve problems

displays a strong knowledge of statistical techniques in solving problems

excels in mathematical calculations

handles mathematical calculations with speed and accuracy

excels in analyzing and adjusting work procedures for maximum efficiency

thoroughly analyzes conditions and reaches independent decisions

concentrates on analyzing essential facts

excels in tedious research

effectively analyzes relevant information

applies sound analytical thinking

excels in analytical thinking

COACHING AND COUNSELING

shows a sincere interest in employees and the solution to their problems

is highly respected by employees for sharing concerns, problems and opportunities

is highly regarded by employees as an excellent counselor

is highly regarded for expert consultation

is well regarded by employees seeking advice

opinions are frequently sought

is an inspiring and influential coach

is a trusted counselor

gives helpful guidance to employees

guides employees to proper resources whenever help is needed

lends support and guidance to employees

inspires voluntary support and guidance to employees

assists employees in career assessment

gives sound practical advice

COACHING AND COUNSELING

demonstrates exceptional skills in employee counseling

effectively uses counseling techniques and skills

uses sound coaching techniques to solve disciplinary problems

excels in effective coaching and counseling of employees

effectively coaches toward achievement

provides continuous coaching

COMMUNICATION SKILLS

excels in effective and positive communications

communicates openly, forcefully and effectively

communicates clearly and concisely

communicates clearly and forcefully

communicates with credibility and confidence

communicates high expectations

effectively communicates expectations

clearly communicates management expectations

improves the effectiveness of communications and interactions with others

provides an intellectual atmosphere conducive to the stimulation and interchange of ideas

excels in interpersonal communications

excels in facilitating group discussions

excels in communicating with individuals and small groups

conducts meetings that achieve results

keeps meetings action-oriented

COMMUNICATION SKILLS

keeps meetings on subject and productive

is a skillful meeting participant

makes a strong impact at meetings

takes an active role in meetings

demonstrates strong committee procedures and techniques

excels in intercommunications and interactions

makes appropriate use of formal vs. informal communications

encourages open communications to achieve mutual understandings

demonstrates an ability to perform and communicate

communicates with strong credibility

is a competent communicator

is a skillful interviewer

asks penetrating questions

is an empathetic listener

prevents unproductive responses

avoids communication breakdowns

(continued)

COMMUNICATION SKILLS

effectively communicates goals and interplay of ideas and concepts

excels in gaining approvals and authorizations

effectively explains and interprets organizational policies and procedures

effectively communicates management decisions to achieve understanding and acceptance

effectively communicates authority under difficult circumstances

communicates effectively with all levels of management

enforces company policies without creating negative reactions

effectively communicates upward, downward and laterally

communicates effectively both horizontally and vertically

develops and maintains two-way communications

keeps other departments informed of developments affecting their functions

effectively communicates with co-workers

communicates confidently with superiors, peers and subordinates

excels in relating well to others

optimally utilizes all channels of communications

demonstrates good judgment in selecting the proper mode of communications

makes effective use of the telephone, fax machine and electronic mail

knows when to cover topics by letter, e-mail, phone or fax

demonstrates proper telephone techniques and etiquette

effectively translates complex information into common terms

is able to communicate complex information in user-friendly terms

responds quickly to all oral and written communications

promptly responds to requests

excels in verbal and nonverbal communications

is able to communicate effectively in other languages

(continued)

COMMUNICATION SKILLS

uses proper oral and written language

possesses a strong vocabulary

displays productive assertiveness

is assertive without being overly aggressive

makes the best impression in all situations

conveys an impression which reflects favorably upon the public relations of the organization

excels in dealing with the public

uses communication skills to bolster the organization's image

is a respected representative of the organization

promotes organizational policies, the quality of its products and its reputation

demonstrates and conveys a favorable image of the organization

COMPETENCY

demonstrates competent performance

displays distinctive competence

projects a special competence

focuses on core competencies

demonstrates a high level of expertise

demonstrates strong personal effectiveness

demonstrates strong interpersonal competence

believes in self

is very confident of abilities

displays accurate self-perception of abilities

uses abilities to the fullest

excels in the effective application of skills

demonstrates highly sophisticated skills and
strategies

possesses specialized skills

highly skilled in all phases of job

excels in operational skills

especially effective in the development and use
of supportive skills

(continued)

COMPETENCY

continuously sharpens and updates skills

is uniquely qualified

is eminently qualified

effectively capitalizes on strengths

accentuates strengths

maximizes personal strengths

devotes appropriate time and effort to the development of professional competence

attends seminars and workshops to improve personal competence

COMPUTER SKILLS

possesses a strong knowledge of computer fundamentals

is strong in computer fundamentals

is strong in computer expertise

excels in converting common tasks to computer processing

is able to skillfully transfer manual functions to computerized systems

is computer literate

takes full advantage of computer programs to maximize productivity

ensures that computers are used to generate meaningful information and increase efficiency

utilizes the power of computers

understands computer applications

makes full use of software capabilities

excels in creating user-friendly programs

maximizes the benefits of computer techniques

capably identifies computer support requirements

(continued)

COMPUTER SKILLS

makes effective use of computer equipment and facilities

keeps alert to new computer hardware

keeps abreast of new software applications

makes effective use of on-line resources

is skillful in navigating the Internet to provide essential information

understands and effectively utilizes the World Wide Web

makes effective use of the World Wide Web

is very knowledgeable in the intricacies of the Internet

makes innovative use of the Internet

is highly skilled in navigating the Internet to find relevant information

excels in diagnosing and solving computer malfunctions

demonstrates a strong ability to solve computer problems

displays strong skills in solving hardware and software malfunctions

COMPUTER SKILLS

excels in trouble shooting

encourages employee acceptance and use of computers

excels in overcoming resistance to new uses of information technology

ensures the proper training of computer operators

is a valuable resource for assisting other computer users

excels in assisting others with computer problems

COOPERATION

works well in cooperation with others for the benefit of the organization

encourages cooperative organizational action

encourages organization-wide cooperation

promotes cooperative behavior and team efforts

develops a strong working rapport with others

builds strong working relationships

is extremely cooperative with associates

gladly shares expertise

shares ideas and techniques

gets along well with others

works effectively with others

is cooperative and open-minded in working with others

works harmoniously and effectively with staff members

inspires cooperation and confidence

is cooperative and constructive

COOPERATION

competes and cooperates

builds cooperation

promotes productive cooperation

receives and carries out tasks in a cooperative manner

effectively implements plans with harmony and cooperation

displays a harmonious and cooperative spirit

is skillful in bringing uncooperative workers together in a spirit of cooperation

COST MANAGEMENT

effectively controls costs through economical utilization of personnel, materials and equipment

effectively commits resources of staff, funds and time

makes maximum use of allocated funds

demonstrates strong budgeting skills

applies strong accounting principles in preparing budgets

makes realistic budget projections

establishes realistic budget objectives

makes operating decisions in conformance with budget limitations

effectively manages departmental budget

deals promptly and effectively with budget variances

gives close attention to monitoring budget variances and plans appropriate adjustments

closely monitors both fixed and variable costs

demonstrates good judgment in making financial decisions

COST MANAGEMENT

strives for maximum return on investment

gives careful attention to cost implications of decisions

is very cost conscious

recognizes the financial implication of all management decisions

excels in profit-oriented decisions

is skillful in developing techniques to improve profitability

is highly competent in analyzing financial information

displays a good working knowledge of cost accounting fundamentals

demonstrates a strong ability to strengthen cost-profit ratios

deals effectively with fiscal restraints

demonstrates sound cost effectiveness

develops strong cost control measures to ensure desired results

excels in developing sound controls for greater cost efficiency

(continued)

COST MANAGEMENT

is very effective in monitoring cost constraints

strictly enforces cost justifications

sets realistic cost priorities

sets effective cost priorities

is very accurate in estimating costs

maintains effective cost control

exercises appropriate cost control

excels in uncovering hidden cost savings

effectively identifies areas needing cost reductions

takes effective measures to achieve cost containment

excels in identifying and controlling critical cost elements

effectively identifies relevant costs

displays sound judgment in managing and controlling expenses

is keenly aware of the impact of expenses on profits

closely monitors expenses and receipts

COST MANAGEMENT

controls expenses without lowering accomplishments

closely tracks all expenses

plans travel, entertainment and related expenses to achieve essential organizational goals

adheres closely to organizational policies and procedures when requesting expense reimbursement

is very conscious of the need for cost justification

ensures that all expenditures are in the best interests of the organization

gives sound consideration to costs when procuring materials and supplies

maintains close inventory control to reduce costs

achieves cost reductions through improved scheduling of personnel

demonstrates success in reducing costs while maintaining high quality

excels in reducing costs

excels in waste reduction management

(continued)

COST MANAGEMENT

demonstrates strong efforts to eliminate waste

excels in controlling costs and eliminating waste

is very effective in controlling waste and spoilage

is very effective in developing internal cost control systems

excels in developing effective audit controls

is very effective in developing and implementing operational audits

implements sound audit controls

adheres to sound ethical and auditing principles

CREATIVITY

displays creative imagination

displays active imagination

demonstrates imaginative insight

provides valuable insights

demonstrates creative strength

successfully develops creative strategies

excels in creative experimentation

is continuously experimenting

seeks creative alternatives

challenges conventional practices

follows a variety of approaches in activities and techniques

explores new paths, procedures and approaches

excels in developing new perspectives

excels in creative thinking and problem solving

is clever and imaginative when confronted with obstacles

(continued)

CREATIVITY

is able to develop creative solutions to challenging problems

develops creative solutions to problems

creates satisfying solutions in conformance with organizational policies

is very creative in developing unique courses of action

demonstrates a high degree of originality and creativity

originates and develops constructive ideas

initiates good conceptual ideas with practical applications

excels in developing spontaneous ideas

originates unsought ideas

seeks new ideas and approaches

stimulates ideas

promotes the flow of good ideas

excels in releasing the creativity of employees

welcomes ideas from subordinates

is receptive to new ideas

CREATIVITY

generates fresh ideas

excels in nurturing new ideas

initiates fresh ideas

discovers new approaches

displays a sense of inquiry

maintains a high level of curiosity

displays a strong power of observation

encourages an environment for creative
excellence

promotes an environment conducive to
creativity

is heavily relied upon for creative support

provides a broad range of creative services

taps the creative potential of a group

promotes a creative climate

creates interest

creates unique value

creates opportunities

DECISION MAKING

makes decisions with confidence

displays firmness in making decisions

can be relied on to make sound decisions

makes sound decisions under pressure

makes sound decisions when faced with multi-faceted problems

makes inventive and resourceful decisions

is very skilled in formulating solutions to difficult issues

is willing to make difficult and unpopular decisions

takes decisive action based on well documented facts

assembles all available facts before making decisions

avoids hasty decisions

effectively uses computer simulation to assist in decision making

seeks staff input for decision making

makes sound decisions in the absence of detailed instructions

DECISION MAKING

uses the most penetrating and objective evaluations to arrive at decisions

weighs alternative decisions before taking action

considers all alternatives before making commitments

weighs numerous scenarios before making decisions

excels in considering diversified approaches before taking action

recognizes and carefully weighs management fads before taking action

is able to effectively weigh theoretical versus practical considerations and applications

carefully evaluates alternative risks

practices sound risk taking

is willing to take calculated risks

is eager to take risks

turns risk situations into opportunities

exercises a wide range of decision making control

(continued)

DECISION MAKING

foresees the consequences of decisions

excels in foreseeing the effects of decisions

weighs strategic ramifications of decisions

communicates decisions with confidence

demonstrates an ability to effectively influence key decision makers

concentrates on developing solutions

excels in seeking solutions

develops fresh solutions

excels in suggesting optional solutions

develops resourceful solutions

supports convictions with sufficient force

strives to improve decisiveness

encourages decision making at lowest possible level

DELEGATING

delegates to improve organizational effectiveness

delegates to maximize organizational strengths

recognizes the importance of working through subordinates

encourages delegation

demonstrates effective delegation techniques

effectively delegates responsibility

gives subordinates the authority needed to effectively carry out delegated responsibilities

empowers employees with the authority and resources to achieve results

excels in empowering team members with responsibility and authority

delegates with clearly defined responsibility and authority

provides subordinates with the resources needed to accomplish results

delegates while maintaining control

knows when and what to delegate

delegates routine tasks to subordinates

(continued)

DELEGATING

makes effective use of secretarial support

delegates to match personal strengths

matches assignments with employee talents

delegates to the proper person

effectively delegates unpleasant tasks

encourages subordinates to solve their own problems

prevents reverse delegation

may be delegated the broadest discretion

delegates to evaluate employee potential

effectively assesses delegation capability

delegates to improve job satisfaction of subordinates

delegates to motivate

delegates to build subordinates

helps subordinates gain visibility

creates a high degree of trust with subordinates

DEPENDABILITY

s consistent, dependable and accurate in
carrying out responsibilities to a successful
conclusion

displays industriousness, conscientiousness
and diligence in performing tasks

can be relied upon to meet schedules and
deadlines

ully accepts all responsibilities and meets
deadlines

verbal commitments are consistent with actions

achieves results when confronted with major
responsibilities and limited resources

utilizes all available resources to achieve
results

can be counted on to achieve results in
emergency situations

is exceptionally reliable and trustworthy when
given an assignment

uses proven methods and techniques to
achieve results

generates greater success in highly complex
situations

displays rigid self-discipline

(continued)

DEPENDABILITY

attains results regardless of task levels

meets responsibilities promptly

fulfills all commitments

meets expectations

is very dependable and conscientious

is a strong and reliable member of the
department

is extremely reliable and supportive

can be trusted to provide support

can be relied upon to accomplish the best
possible results

can be relied upon to do the job and any other
assigned tasks

is always fully prepared

can be relied upon to successfully complete all
assignments

consistently punctual

is regular in attendance

effectively follows-up assignments

DEVELOPMENT

xcels in selecting and developing individuals
ith high potential talent

xcels in recognizing employees with strong
rowth potential

fast developing a department known for its
redibility

lentifies staff development needs

ecognizes development levels and ability
vels of staff . . . and others

xcels in orienting new employees

itiates and establishes personal growth and
areer paths

xcels in developing career paths

lans for effective career development

lans for future career development and
ccomplishment

hows a strong interest in professional
evelopment

eager to participate in professional
evelopment programs

eeks personal growth and development

(continued)

DEVELOPMENT

understands personal strengths and weaknesses

regularly assesses the development and effectiveness of subordinates

inspires subordinates to achieve their fullest potential

excels in developing mutual expectations

encourages broad development of employees

makes effective use of lateral transfers to offer fresh challenges

shows genuine interest in employee progress

effectively tracks employee progress

deals effectively with different career stages of employees

encourages individual growth and development of employees

excels in identifying individual strengths

excels in tapping hidden talents

excels in developing hidden strengths of employees

exploits under-utilized capabilities

DEVELOPMENT

maximizes employees' energy and capabilities

displays an ability to turn weaknesses into strengths

develops subordinates into high achievers

cultivates strengths of subordinates

brings out the best in employees

effectively develops employees

develops managerial candidates

produces many managers

encourages managers to develop subordinates

excels in developing synergy

gives proper attention to personnel succession planning

develops qualified successors

encourages employees to acquire proper skills, attitudes and knowledge

makes accurate assessments of training needs

encourages special preparation and training of personnel

uses a wide variety of training methods (continued)

DEVELOPMENT

develops innovative and powerful training techniques

is very proficient in both on-the-job and classroom training

makes effective use of role playing

improves the skills and develops talents of subordinates

successfully builds subordinates

encourages employees to improve abilities for greater responsibility

encourages employees to strive for continuous improvement

encourages employees to become promotable

excels in developing marginal employees

effectively recommends methods to assist subordinates in overcoming weaknesses

concentrates development on weak areas

encourages constructive actions by employees

makes strong efforts to bring out the best in every employee

Assists subordinates in reaching new levels of skills, knowledge and attitudes

makes winners out of subordinates

Assists subordinates in applying new skills, techniques and understandings

creates a desire to learn

facilitates learning

develops creative potential

profits from experience

builds on strengths

reinforces positive behavior

reinforces employee strengths

builds on the positive

ENVIRONMENTAL, SAFETY AND SECURITY

keeps abreast of all environmental concerns

displays a strong awareness of environmental concerns

closely enforces all government environmental regulations

follows sound environmental practices

closely adheres to all environmental policies concerning discharges, emissions and exposure

takes proper measures to avoid spills and releases

is skillful in training employees for emergencies

is careful to follow proper storage procedures

complies with all safety recommendations and requirements

closely follows all safety regulations

keeps well informed of safety requirements

makes certain that all safety regulations are adhered to

places a high priority on workplace safety

shows concern for worker safety

ENVIRONMENTAL, SAFETY AND SECURITY

is very safety conscious

excels in accident prevention management

makes effective use of safety awards and incentives

is a strong supporter and participant in safety training programs

keeps alert for all job hazards

takes prompt action to eliminate work hazards

takes prompt action to eliminate unsafe conditions

promptly reports suspicious activities to security personnel

closely follows all security measures

adheres to all security policies

EVALUATION SKILLS

establishes clear and meaningful criteria or standards for effective performance

clearly establishes performance objectives and evaluation criteria

develops key performance factors for fair comparisons

establishes credible standards

establishes credible measurement methods

effectively and continuously evaluates activities, programs and functions

continuously evaluates techniques and practices

effectively appraises departmental resources and skills

accurately monitors performance against objectives

effectively makes quantitative determinations of ability

recognizes high potential employees

identifies individuals who have a capacity to perform

effectively identifies goal achievers

EVALUATION SKILLS

produces highly accurate assessments

provides management with accurate information concerning the strengths and weaknesses of employees

effectively assesses employee resources, strengths and competencies

regularly assesses growth

effectively tracks performance

accurately assesses potential

accurately evaluates employee effectiveness

effectively assesses the quality of work performed by subordinates

rates on the basis of performance and not personality

effectively rates job performance and not the individual

carefully limits all evaluations to on-the-job performance

effectively evaluates subordinates on the basis of performance

distinguishes between ability and actual performance

(continued)

EVALUATION SKILLS

effectively documents observations with specific examples

recognizes the need for accurate documentation in the evaluation process

skillfully documents performance

ensures that all criticism is fully documented

effectively evaluates others without creating resentment or negative responses

shows significant frequency differences in appraising employees

gives recognition to deserving individuals

is quick to recognize extra efforts

effectively grants rewards on the basis of objective accomplishment

assigns salary increases based on true performance

clearly identifies the main attributes of strong performers

recognizes special talents and capabilities of employees

understands accomplishments, strengths and weaknesses of employees

identifies individuals needing periodic retraining

EVALUATION SKILLS

identifies and discusses weaknesses of staff members

directs performance appraisals toward the self-improvement of employee

effectively uses performance reviews as a motivational tool

makes effective use of performance evaluations to inspire greater achievements

plans for appraisal interview

gives proper attention to performance appraisal interviews

anticipates employee reactions to appraisal interview

prepares for possible negative reaction to evaluation review

encourages and facilitates self-evaluation

effectively critiques own work

benefits from constructive criticism

excels in establishing feedback systems for evaluating results

accurately measures and assesses employee feedback

GOALS AND OBJECTIVES

excels in planning, forecasting, setting objectives and determining courses of action

effectively develops individual, departmental and organizational goals to attain objectives

effectively blends personal goals with organizational objectives

sets goals that are compatible with those of the organization

excels in formulating goals and plans of action

clearly establishes goals to achieve a significant productive impact

effectively sets optimal targets

establishes performance targets for both short-range and long-range

sets, obtains and manages managerial objectives

sets innovative objectives

formulates realistic objectives

establishes specific objectives

effectively determines workable objectives

excels in the perception of objectives

GOALS AND OBJECTIVES

encompasses every objective valued by the organization

effectively communicates objectives

effectively develops objectives

achieves cognitive objectives

establishes feasible and attainable goals

sets realistic goals

sets reachable targets

sets high standards of personal performance

sets compelling personal goals

sets worthy goals

effectively develops goals

is a goal seeker

clearly establishes goals and purposes

effectively establishes truly relevant objectives and performance standards

establishes specific and measurable goals

sets clear and measurable objectives

(continued)

GOALS AND OBJECTIVES

effectively sets group performance objectives

effectively establishes group goals

establishes methods for attainment of goals

effectively organizes, assembles and arranges resources to meet goals

is aware of longer-term goals and larger framework of concepts

effectively evaluates goals

displays sincerity of ambitions and objectives

keeps employees focused on achieving goals

uses goals to maintain momentum

achieves and surpasses goals

IMPROVEMENT

continuously strives to strengthen and refine professional effectiveness

continuously seeks higher levels of expertise

consistently strives to improve performance

strives for personal enrichment

is continuously planning for improvement

sustains continuous improvement

moves constructively toward improving performance

excels in enhancing performance

improves effectiveness by eliminating the confusing

excels in self-supervision and self-improvement

promotes improvement-oriented ideas

often makes valuable suggestions for improvement

develops continuous improvement methods

excels in developing improved techniques

develops totally new strategies

(continued)

IMPROVEMENT

devises improved means of accomplishing results

is a major contributor to organization improvement

produces changes for the overall improvement of the department

displays a willingness to discuss weaknesses and make improvements

promptly corrects shortcomings of subordinates

uses constructive criticism to improve performance

establishes goals for improvement of performance targets

develops future goals for self-improvement

articulates goals for future improvement

sets ambitious growth goals

tactfully discusses areas in need of improvement

clearly identifies improvements to be achieved

works cooperatively toward the identification of areas needing improvements

IMPROVEMENT

establishes clear expectations

focuses on areas having the greatest potential for improvement

excels in isolating characteristics in need of improvement

clearly pinpoints areas of needed improvements

identifies performance improvement problems

monitors improvement progress

displays an eagerness to improve

demonstrates a strong effort to improve

welcomes opportunities for improvement

seeks opportunities for self-improvement

seeks continuous improvement

seeks feed-back to improve performance

responds favorably to suggested actions for improvement

displays improved potential for advancement

shows steady progress

continues to grow and improve

INITIATIVE

demonstrates a high level of initiative

is a self-starter

is judicious in carrying out assignments without direction

excels in self-directing and self-pacing

demonstrates an ability to think along constructive original lines

is a solution seeker

takes the initiative in solving problems

effectively initiates solutions

makes practical suggestions

displays self-reliant enterprise

excels in identifying new areas of opportunities

keeps alert to greater opportunities

is alert to new opportunities, techniques and approaches

is eager to take on new assignments

seizes all opportunities

INITIATIVE

explores new opportunities

captures all opportunities

effectively applies new concepts and techniques

continuously finds new and better ways of performing job

extremely active and eager to try new approaches

displays ingenuity in anticipating and meeting unexpected situations

provides opportunities for initiative

gathers and provides data in advance of need

plans and organizes with little or no assistance

takes action without undue haste or delay

does things without being told

has the quality of knowing what has to be done

takes charge in the absence of detailed instructions

requires minimum supervision

INNOVATION

excels in developing innovative and creative solutions

seeks innovative solutions

develops innovative plans and solutions

innovates and creates new and unique methods and procedures

excels in innovative thinking

considers innovative possibilities

fosters a curiosity for innovative possibilities

seeks continuous innovation

encourages innovation

promotes innovation

develops innovative strategies

develops innovative approaches

demonstrates innovative insight

is extremely innovative under adverse conditions

is very innovative when confronted with limited resources

INTERPERSONAL SKILLS

excels in effective human relations

understands human behavior

identifies and understands personal values of superiors, subordinates, peers and others

recognizes the needs of others

displays a high degree of recognition, acceptance and prestige in dealing with others

makes favorable impression and easily gains acceptance by others

recognizes the importance of first impressions

is quick to gain recognition and respect

conveys a positive personal image

excels in obtaining enthusiastic commitments

gains management commitments

well accepted by others under difficult circumstances

develops positive working relationships

develops mutual support

is able to quickly establish rapport

(continued)

INTERPERSONAL SKILLS

builds a close rapport

builds trust and rapport

builds a climate of trust

excels in trust building

promotes relationships of trust and respect

develops interpersonal trust

develops relationships based on dependability and honesty

builds on mutual dependence and understanding

understands and knows how to get along with co-workers

establishes effective working relationships

promotes harmony among associates

attracts the favorable attention of superiors

builds positive relationships with superiors

works effectively with multiple superiors

conveys considerable influence with superiors

exercises considerable influence

INTERPERSONAL SKILLS

establishes credibility with superiors and subordinates

interacts effectively with peers

displays unconditional positive regard

conveys positive influences

displays genuineness in dealing with others

conveys a willingness to help

generates synergy

promotes participative approaches

demonstrates an ability to relate

excels in sustaining concentration while avoiding confrontations

demonstrates strong interpersonal skills

displays an interpersonal regard

displays positive effectivity

respects the opinions of others

JUDGMENT

makes wise and fair judgments based on solid facts

can be trusted to use good judgment

is very open-minded in judgmental situations

is open-minded when forming opinions

excels in making appropriate judgments

draws sound conclusions

makes thoughtful determinations

displays excellent intuitive judgment

exercises careful deliberations before making judgments

gives thoughtful consideration before forming opinions

weighs alternative courses of action

systematically evaluates options in terms of consequences

effectively diagnoses situations or conditions

is not governed by conventional wisdom

exercises sound judgment on behalf of others

KNOWLEDGE

knows basic management principles and methods

possesses the knowledge to handle work of the most complex nature

clearly understands purposes, objectives, practices and procedures of department

displays strong knowledge of responsibilities

thoroughly understands all aspects of job

understands needs and requirements of job

is secure in job knowledge

is very knowledgeable over a wide range of job responsibilities

has excellent "real world" experience

possesses practical hands-on experience

demonstrates a strong, functional knowledge

displays a broad application of knowledge

is exceptionally well informed

shares knowledge for the benefit of employees

keeps alert to current practices

(continued)

KNOWLEDGE

recognizes the power of information

demonstrates a tremendous knowledge of resources

possesses an invaluable source of knowledge

demonstrates a comprehensive knowledge of the field

is a preeminent authority

keeps informed of the latest trends and developments

keeps well informed on business, political and social issues

keeps well informed of pertinent legislation and regulations

keeps fully abreast of changing government regulations

excels in gaining knowledge through continuous study

LEADERSHIP

projects self-confidence, authority and enthusiasm

displays the confidence needed to face the toughest leadership challenges

is successfully meeting the position's leadership challenges

demonstrates natural leadership ability

displays a strong ability to lead and direct

displays leadership stature

demonstrates strong, dynamic leadership

shows dynamic leadership qualities

is a charismatic leader

is able to quickly create rapport

is able to quickly gain the support of others

displays the strengths of the exceptional leader

demonstrates imaginative leadership

displays strong leadership patterns

displays many leadership competencies

displays leadership traits appropriate to the situation

(continued)

LEADERSHIP

possesses essential leadership traits

excels in training, leading and motivating people

conveys an authoritative image that commands respect

effectively uses power and influence

knows when to restrain and when to exercise power

commands a high degree of influence

is able to assert authority when challenged

is willing to challenge conventional wisdom

radiates authority

demonstrates decisive leadership ability

faces problems with confidence and assurance

inspires confidence and respect

inspires distinguished performance

is an inspirational leader

is a catalyst for success

radiates confidence

LEADERSHIP

elicits confidence

takes a leadership role in group situations

effectively maintains leadership in a group environment

takes charge

leads by example

is emulated by peers and subordinates

displays an ability to stimulate others

inspires others to do their best

commands the respect of others

displays a strong ability to build credibility

earns the respect and loyalty of subordinates

leads with authority and respect

is a trusted leader

is quick to gain the trust of others

commands undivided attention

commands the attention of others

maintains a high profile in the organization

(continued)

LEADERSHIP

is widely recognized as a strong leader

shows appreciation for contributions and achievements

inspires new employees to become leaders

promotes a high degree of morale

strengthens morale

promotes harmony and teamwork

promotes group harmony

promotes a common purpose

creates shared drive and purpose

LEARNING ABILITY

shows eagerness and capacity to learn

learning capacity is exceptional

is eager to enhance skill levels

displays an exceptional ability to learn new methods

displays an ability to learn rapidly and adapt quickly to changing situations

responds promptly to changes and opportunities

responds quickly to new instructions, situations, methods and procedures

displays a short learning curve

quickly grasps new routines and explanations

is receptive to new ideas

keeps alert to new learning opportunities

uses sound techniques to maximize learning

makes effective use of hands-on learning

learns quickly from setbacks

benefits from all learning situations

(continued)

LEARNING ABILITY

shares learning experience with subordinates

encourages a positive learning environment

promotes a learning climate

stimulates curiosity to improve learning

makes a strong effort to maintain new skills

is committed to continuous learning

is continuously learning through educational and professional improvement programs

LOYALTY AND DEDICATION

places a high priority on loyalty and dedication

encourages loyalty throughout the organization

displays strong loyalty to superiors and to the organization

is loyal to organization, associates and subordinates

builds loyalty in subordinates

expects strong loyalty

builds loyalty at every opportunity

displays a high degree of honesty, loyalty and integrity

displays loyalty to profession

is a strong supporter of all organizational programs and activities

displays a genuine interest in the organization

is committed to organizational goals

takes pride in contributing to the organization's success

takes pride in job

increases superior's strengths

(continued)

LOYALTY AND DEDICATION

shows positive attitudes toward employer and employees

is extremely dedicated

is totally committed to achieving excellence

projects a renewed sense of purpose

is highly devoted to achieving objectives

is highly committed to achieving organizational success

MANAGEMENT
ABILITY

effectively applies sound management
principles

is building a solid management foundation for
future growth

effectively uses contemporary management
concepts

demonstrates productive management
techniques

encourages participative management

stimulates management efficiency and
effectiveness

multiplies management effectiveness

successfully integrates objectives,
opportunities and resources

is a powerful asset to the organization

develops sensible and realistic programs

orchestrates successful programs

successfully builds and reinforces essential
programs

identifies major management problems

demonstrates an ability to recognize
management problems and develop solutions

(continued)

MANAGEMENT ABILITY

knows when to seek help outside the organization

identifies relevant and appraisable components of effective management

accurately assesses management effectiveness

keeps management informed on questions of policy

excels in obtaining management support

consistently prepares appropriate recommendations

displays strength in human resources management

excels in human resources management

provides management with valid and reliable information for human resources planning

effectively resolves conflicts between individual needs and requirements of the organization

respects both employee rights and management prerogatives

demonstrates an ability to overcome internal barriers

effectively solves problems that cross organizational boundaries

excels in resolving interdepartmental conflicts

obtains full commitments throughout the organization

obtains the full support of other departments

pulls the organization together

recognizes the important roles of responsibility, authority and accountability

establishes accountability throughout the organization

demands accountability from subordinates

holds subordinates accountable for results

relates consequences to accountability

is a polished and effective executive

demonstrates superior executive ability under a variety of circumstances

conveys executive stature

conveys an executive presence

displays executive strength

(continued)

MANAGEMENT ABILITY

shows those qualities that make a manager forceful and effective

displays attributes of an effective manager

shows strong self-management

effectively manages self

displays an effective, productive management style

recognizes the differences between managing and doing

avoids managing by crisis

is a challenging and inspiring manager

excels in solving people problems

excels in defining, measuring and increasing productivity

achieves high productive output while maintaining high morale

builds organizational harmony

keeps employees aware of their importance to the organization

encourages efforts toward common goals

excels in developing synergistic strategies

accounts for effective and efficient use of personnel

provides subordinates with the resources needed to attain results

attains results through the proper direction of subordinates

excels in managing distant employees

gives clear direction

avoids overstepping authority

develops a cohesive department effort

is aware of potential contributions of department

maintains firm departmental control

adheres to all policies, procedures and rules of decorum

effectively enforces policies, rules and regulations

is effective in taking measures to reduce the organization's exposure to litigation

(continued)

MANAGEMENT ABILITY

ensures that all policies are accurate, thoroughly documented and consistently applied

maintains high ethical standards

displays sound ethics

follows proper codes of conduct

effectively recognizes the need for change

effectively manages change

provides a stabilizing influence during periods of organizational change

implements change with minimal resistance

is able to break through barriers of resistance when implementing changes

is able to implement change in a reluctant environment

effectively deals with resistance to change

implements change with a positive impact

keeps fully alert to the weaknesses, strengths, threats and opportunities facing the organization

excels in positioning for the future

MATURITY

displays a high degree of emotional maturity

excels in separating emotion from rationality

displays emotional stability

displays strong emotional control

avoids emotional involvement

copes constructively with emotions

avoids overreacting

keeps anger under control

confronts reality

displays mature reactions

maintains a mature attitude

maintains strong self-control

displays superior emotional adjustments and stability

recovers promptly from unfortunate circumstances

displays maturity in handling disappointments

responds positively on inconsequential issues

MENTAL SKILLS

grasps the most difficult concepts

displays a depth of understanding

understands both theoretical and practical concepts

excels in both theoretical and practical thinking

is capable of preparing highly complex statistical data

distinguishes between perception and reality

exceptionally keen and alert

is reasonable, smart and keen

is alert, quick and responsive

is alert and broad-minded

keeps alert to strategic opportunities

capable of sustaining a high level of concentration

is able to focus on a single task until completion

gives undivided attention

is not governed by conventional thinking

MENTAL SKILLS

is continuously rethinking traditional assumptions

demonstrates original and independent thinking

sustains logical thinking in one area

thinks before taking action

thinks fast on feet

uses common sense

uses common sense to reach workable conclusions

uses sound fact-finding approaches

displays fresh insights

is skillful in developing practical insights

uses intelligent reasoning

demonstrates sound inductive and deductive reasoning

displays considerable flexibility

displays strong mental flexibility

exhibits mental toughness when necessary

(continued)

MENTAL SKILLS

displays fresh thinking

displays imaginative thinking

displays organized thinking

excels in divergent thinking

excels in heuristic thinking

excels in independent thinking

thinks strategically

displays consistent, logical and orderly thinking

displays excellent comprehension and retention

displays a high level of knowledge retention

displays strong powers of mental retention

excels in retaining and recalling information

possesses strong memory skills

displays strong memory power

displays a strong power of recall

possesses a strong ability to remember and recall

MENTAL SKILLS

displays a remarkable power to remember details

possesses multilingual skills

is able to understand and speak in other languages

displays a very high cognitive ability

excels in systematic observation

displays strong powers of observation

gains new perspectives

demonstrates intellectual inquisitiveness

widens intellectual horizons

makes effective use of mental imaging

demonstrates positive mental outlook

recognizes the growing importance of global thinking

thinks futuristically

MOTIVATION

strongly motivated to achieve optimal results

strongly motivated to achieve higher expectations

displays a strong incentive to succeed

highly motivated to achieve individual attainment

strives for the achievement of excellence

strives for maximum effectiveness

is very performance conscious

displays maximum drive fulfilling job responsibilities

is a significant driving force

keeps drive alive

maintains a high level of readiness for action

displays a strong sense of purpose

displays a sustained commitment

displays a strong personal commitment

demonstrates a high level of commitment

displays strong achievement drive

provides a competitive edge

displays a strong competitive drive

turns competitive impulses into the most constructive channels

displays intense desire

demonstrates strong will power and determination

displays a spirit of determination

optimizes individual traits

displays highly motivated inner drive

effectively overcomes personal and organizational blocks to achieve results

effectively uses behavior modification to create motivation and achieve results

displays an enthusiastic spirit

is realistically enthusiastic

maintains fresh enthusiasm

displays energy and enthusiasm

works with enthusiasm

(continued)

MOTIVATION

displays extraordinary enthusiasm

generates enthusiasm

sparks enthusiasm

builds employee enthusiasm

develops a motivating environment

motivates and challenges

uses subtle techniques to motivate

accentuates the positive

generates positive attitudes

provides positive reinforcements to achieve
results

uses positive reinforcement to motivate

displays high energy and drive

maintains a high energy level

goes beyond what is expected

gives maximum effort

displays energy and vitality in performing daily
responsibilities

MOTIVATION

displays intense involvement

seeks total involvement

volunteers for extra work and demanding assignments

is totally absorbed in job

turns past failures into future successes

is success-oriented

capitalizes on opportunities

views problems as opportunities

recoils promptly from problems

maximizes opportunities within every situation

operates effectively under adverse conditions

looks beyond obstacles

surmounts obstacles

is able to overcome extreme difficulties

is highly energized

is highly energetic and enterprising

instills energy and enthusiasm

(continued)

MOTIVATION

displays positive energy

is a prime mover

is a compulsive achiever

is ambitious and hard-driving

is ambitious and high-spirited

is task-oriented

is achievement-oriented

is persistent in achieving goals

is results-oriented

displays progressive attributes

is seldom complacent

is not content with mediocrity

is a self-motivator

sustains a high level of momentum

maintains own momentum

maintains self-motivation

makes effective use of positive imagery to
achieve success

NEGOTIATING SKILLS

demonstrates strong negotiating skills

negotiates with skill

displays strength in negotiating

keeps assertiveness and empathy in balance
when negotiating

is an adept negotiator

excels in negotiating fair resolutions

is consistently able to negotiate successful
outcomes

possesses strong facilitation skills

is a key facilitator

effectively resolves misunderstandings

keeps conflicts from arising

excels in resolving conflicts

works well with others in the solution of mutual
problems

presents different opinions without creating
conflicts

reconciles differences without creating
resentment

(continued)

NEGOTIATING SKILLS

effectively handles differing viewpoints

disagrees diplomatically

disagrees without arguing

is skillful in refusing unreasonable demands

knows how and when to say "no"

is able to successfully confront when
necessary

handles confrontations with tact

negotiates with tact

skillfully handles confrontations

is extremely confident in facing confrontations

prepares thoroughly for negotiations

ORAL EXPRESSION

is a polished and confident speaker

is a formidable speaker

is an inspiring speaker

excels in speaking on special occasions

excels in impromptu speaking situations

excels in delivering impromptu remarks

excels in extemporaneous speaking

speaks effectively on feet

communicates with ease and a natural style

is a powerful communicator in group settings

makes a strong impact at meetings

makes effective demonstrations

makes effective use of questions

makes effective use of an extensive vocabulary

possesses superior verbal understanding

uses understandable language that is relevant and meaningful

uses concise and clear language

(continued)

ORAL EXPRESSION

excels in speech proficiency

is eminently clear in verbal expressions

is highly articulate

displays clarity in expressing views

states positions clearly

displays an ability to present views logically

expresses ideas clearly

speaks at a pleasant tempo

enunciates clearly in a well-modulated voice

speaks in a positive tone

speaks with enthusiasm and confidence

makes dynamic impressions

ORGANIZING

effectively develops organizational capabilities and integration of objectives

develops programs to improve the effectiveness of the department and overall operation of the organization

builds organizational effectiveness

excels in developing jobs, organizational structure and systems

keeps organizational levels to a minimum

avoids over-staffing

maximizes organizational productivity

overcomes organizational block-ups

makes the most of organizational energy and potential

makes a substantial contribution to the growth of the organization

exerts a positive influence on the organizational climate

deals effectively with organizational climate

displays a broad grasp of the organization

identifies organizational needs

(continued)

ORGANIZING

encourages accountability throughout the organization

displays an organized approach to the job

organizes work well

organizes effectively to achieve greater results

demonstrates a systematic approach in carrying out assignments

is very orderly and systematic

excels in cutting through confusion

excels in turning chaos into order

makes order out of chaos

is methodical in planning and performing

PERSONAL QUALITIES

is fair, cheerful and follows businesslike procedures to accomplish objectives

recognizes and accepts personal assets and liabilities

recognizes personal limitations

displays a pleasant, cheerful disposition

displays natural charm and charisma

displays a pleasant demeanor

has a calm, even temperament

is stable, patient and steady

is relaxed, confident, enjoyable

is polished and poised

is very cordial

displays social grace

is warm and genuine

is sincere

projects objectivity

avoids unrealistic promises

(continued)

PERSONAL QUALITIES

maintains a sense of humor

uses humor constructively

displays keen wit

possesses a personal magnetism

is quick to build rapport

possesses all traits associated with excellence

possesses many valued personal traits

displays refinement and character

displays many positive character traits

maintains a positive attitude

displays strong moral character

remains steadfast to core beliefs

demonstrates a commitment to core values

is highly regarded for integrity

displays impeccable honesty

is impeccably honest

maintains the highest standards of honesty and ethics

PERSONAL QUALITIES

is highly credible

displays a winning personality

displays a pleasing personality

displays an enterprising personality

displays an outgoing personality

maintains high recognition

displays energizing optimism

displays many action-oriented skills

projects energy and enthusiasm

PERSUASIVENESS

demonstrates strong persuasive power

demonstrates strong persuasive skills

demonstrates excellent persuasive ability

uses chronological reasoning to effectively persuade

uses sound reasoning to effectively persuade

excels in using logical thinking to persuade

effectively persuades using strong arguments

excels in acquiring support for decisions and actions

is very skilled in gaining the support of others

is a strong consensus-builder

is very effective in gaining support for a consensus

excels in gaining support of views and opinions

is able to change the views of others without causing resentment

excels in changing attitudes

reinforces ideas and proposals with sound documentation

PERSUASIVENESS

is very effective in overcoming objections using skillful persuasion

is able to consistently overcome objectives and reach common agreements

persuades without antagonizing

persuades with tact

seeks persuasive challenges

makes persuasive presentations

communicates with persuasion

is very convincing

uses voice and body to effectively convince and persuade

writes with persuasion

PLANNING

establishes strategic plans for future success

proposes plans of action which are timely, realistic and positive

is skillful in developing plans that reflect a consensus of opinion

plans with a fresh perspective

maintains a broad perspective

plans, organizes and completes tasks in the shortest, most efficient manner

effectively formulates strategies, tactics and action plans to achieve results

plans appropriate strategies to arrive at solutions

plans effectively for systematic results

excels in defining problems and planning solutions

meets or exceeds standards for major responsibilities or objectives on time or ahead of schedule

effectively plans work schedules to balance peak and slack periods

keeps comfortably ahead of work schedule

PLANNING

translates planning into reality

develops rational planning techniques

excels in developing tactical action plans

develops sound action plans

develops workable action plans

effectively puts plans into action

makes strategically sound plans

formulates sound strategies

develops comprehensive strategies

excels in formulating and executing strategies

excels in strategy and action

effectively translates ideas into action

is very skilled in turning theory into action
plans

excels in developing strategic aims

excels in anticipatory management

anticipates emerging opportunities

is quick to recognize emerging trends

(continued)

PLANNING

excels in anticipating approaching problems and opportunities

effectively plans to avoid future problems

excels in problem prevention

prevents problems from occurring

excels in anticipating reactions

plans for predictable resistance

anticipates and resolves conflicts

excels in anticipating needs

is adept at assessing needs

makes accurate assessments of needs

excels in projecting resource needs

is highly proficient in scheduling materials, labor and operations

excels in planning, forecasting and replenishing vital needs

develops positive strategies

excels in anticipating approaching problems

PLANNING

Develops effective strategies to attain good performance

Creates flexible plans to meet changing opportunities

Continuously develops techniques to generate new strategic alternatives

Plans for the unexpected

Plans effectively for uncertain conditions

Is very competent in emergency management planning

Excels in developing "what if" scenarios

Excels in developing strategic alternatives

Develops sound contingency plans

Focuses on the future

POTENTIAL

possesses a strong capacity to make a greater contribution to the organization

is capable of distinguished performance in a higher level position

possesses the knowledge, experience and leadership qualities to achieve success at a higher management level

displays high management potential

is a strong contender for a higher position

is strongly qualified for advancement

displays strong potential for advancement

is a strong candidate for advancement

is presently capable of assuming greater responsibility

is qualified for greater responsibility

deserves serious consideration for greater responsibility

is capable of handling bigger projects and assignments

is capable of assuming greater challenges

POTENTIAL

s capable of assuming a greater leadership
role

has reached the level for promotional
consideration

s a high potential employee

s highly promotable

needs more responsibility to ensure continued
satisfaction and career growth

s capable of assuming greater responsibility in
present position

present position provides ample opportunity for
growth

responsibilities are being gradually increased
to improve advancement potential

s a high potential employee with broad and
solid experience

displays a high energy potential

displays a strong capacity for growth

possesses many latent strengths

turns potential into action

is highly motivated for greater opportunities

(continued)

POTENTIAL

is eager to demonstrate greater potential

displays a strong desire for advancement

is eager to assume greater responsibility in the department or elsewhere

is capable of managing a larger department

is making a strong effort to acquire greater experience and skills to increase potential for advancement

is enhancing growth potential through additional education and training

PRESENTATION SKILLS

demonstrates excellent oral presentation skills

demonstrates strong personal presentation skills

is a skillful presenter

is a recognized and highly regarded presenter

makes presentations with poise and confidence

makes presentations with grace and style

delivers presentations with enthusiasm and energy

makes lively and effective presentations

makes presentations that are interesting and lively

creates indelible impressions when making presentations

makes effective use of body language

delivers presentations with maximum impact

makes presentations that deliver a powerful message

makes powerful presentations

prepares persuasive presentations

(continued)

PRESENTATION SKILLS

faces any size audience with confidence

makes outstanding presentations to management

is able to gain the respect of audiences

is skilled in capturing the interests and involvement of audiences

is skilled in engaging audience participation

excels in directing audience participation

responds effectively to difficult questions and opposing views

skillfully handles unanticipated questions

effectively organizes ideas for logical presentation and acceptance

communicates effectively with well designed materials

presentations are well prepared

presentations are well researched and highly credible

uses visual aids effectively

makes effective use of charts, graphs, figures and illustrations

PRESENTATION SKILLS

s very skilled at preparing cost effective in-
house presentations

excels in developing and using computer
generated presentations

excels in making powerful presentations using
computer graphics

s very skilled in making excellent use of presentation software

s skilled in making presentations for video
taping

s able to effectively present dry and technical
information

excels in presenting complex information and
technical data

continuously strives to improve presentation skills

PRIORITIZING

is able to successfully prioritize when faced with requests, demands and deadlines

displays a strong sense of priorities

keeps situations in proper perspective

excels in priority determinations

excels in prioritizing objectives

excels in priority management

keeps focused on relevant policy issues

effectively handles competing priorities

effectively copes with competing priorities

capably prioritizes the demands of multiple superiors

meets logically developed priorities

concentrates on activities with a high payoff

concentrates on activities with the greatest payback

focuses on relevant issues

focuses on essential activities

focuses time and energy on meaningful activities

PRIORITIZING

distinguishes between low and high priority activities

identifies unessential activities

excels in eliminating unproductive activities

focuses on value added activities

effectively distinguishes between value and non-valued activities

excels in eliminating all activities not creating value

effectively establishes task priorities

eliminates tasks which contribute the least to organizational goals

recognizes the need to concentrate on people rather than tasks

is able to distinguish between the crucial and trivial

avoids useless trivia

sees the big picture

effectively prioritizes daily and weekly activities

places organizational needs ahead of personal convenience

PROBLEM SOLVING

demonstrates a strong ability to identify, analyze and solve problems

displays an ability to solve problems, think, reason and learn

is skilled in identifying and solving bottlenecks

develops non-traditional solutions

excels in developing viable solutions

is skilled in proposing optional solutions

excels in developing alternative solutions

develops creative and cost effective solutions

excels in creative problem solving

develops satisfying solutions

makes a strong effort to be a part of the solution

develops cohesive solutions that benefit the entire organization

displays a practical approach to solving problems

uses the latest technologies to improve operations and overcome problems

PROBLEM SOLVING

unusually decisive in handling difficult problems

effectively solves problems rather than symptoms

keeps informed of developing problems

is quick to identify problems

excels in identifying real problems

focuses on core problems

excels in solving critical problems

excels in solving multi-faceted problems

solves problems before they become critical

is quick to resolve and overcome obstacles

effectively resolves problems at early stages

excels in trouble shooting

works well with others in solving problems

translates problems into practical solutions

looks upon problems as exciting challenges

turns problems into opportunities

PRODUCTIVITY

makes a substantial contribution to the continued operation and growth of the organization

is an important contributor to the successes of the department

is a proven performer

demonstrates consistently distinguished performance

quantity of work is consistently high

performs at peak efficiency

maintains a peak performance

sustains a high achievement level

works at a high achievement level

performs at a high energy level

effectively expends energy

maintains unusually high output

is fast and productive

performs with unusual speed at a high rate of output

exceeds normal output standards

PRODUCTIVITY

produces measurable results

is an abundant producer

consistently exceeds performance expectations

produces beyond normal expectations

performance regularly exceeds job requirements

continuously produces more than expected

PROFESSIONALISM

demonstrates an exceptional mastery of professional skills

is at the pinnacle of professional excellence

demonstrates professional expertise

displays well-oriented professional knowledge

communicates on a high professional level

is a seasoned professional

seeks a higher degree of professional excellence

is eager to build professional credentials

welcomes professional challenges

shows concern about professional improvement

sustains a professional growth strategy

strives to grow professionally through continuous study and participation

closely follows professional trends

continuously seeks to broaden professional horizons

knows when to bring in outside expertise

PROFESSIONALISM

maintains a high degree of professional participation

develops the skills needed to maintain the highest standards of professional excellence

quality of work reflects high professional standards

displays high standards of professional behavior

demonstrates high standards of professional conduct

possesses high professional values

maintains the highest standards of ethics

maintains high professional ethics

follows high ethical practices

follows ethical procedures

maintains a high degree of ethical conduct

displays a high level of personal integrity

provides subordinates with definite, positive assistance to correct professional difficulties

develops enduring professional relationships

stimulates professionalism

(continued)

PROFESSIONALISM

conveys professionalism

displays loyalty to profession

engenders respect for profession

displays a professional style

displays professional pride

makes excellent impressions

projects a positive image

projects poise and authority

conforms to proper standards of professional dress

dresses appropriately for the position consistent with job requirements

wears appropriate clothing and accessories consistent with job requirements

dresses consistent with organizational expectations

dresses to convey an appropriate image in accordance with position requirements

writing reflects a polished professional appearance

writes memos, letters and reports that reflect professional expertise plans, organizes and completes projects in the shortest, most efficient manner

completes the most complex projects with impressive results

clearly establishes project goals and objectives

demonstrates a systematic approach in carrying out projects

handles projects in logical sequence

excels in obtaining management support for projects

excels in building a powerful project management team

makes effective use of all available resources when given a project

sets realistic timetables to keep projects on target

effectively tracks the progress of various projects

keeps projects on schedule and within budget

excels in vitalizing stalled projects

is able to keep programs and projects running smoothly

(continued)

PROJECT MANAGEMENT

successfully handles multiple projects at the same time

accepts special projects with enthusiasm

is eager to accept challenging projects

is exceptionally reliable when given a project

displays a strong personal commitment to successfully completing all projects

keeps management fully informed of a project's progress

writes reports that contain solid findings and recommendations

makes excellent presentations of completed projects

QUALITY

promotes quality values throughout the organization

effectively uses empowerment to achieve improved quality

recognizes the importance of quality in providing a competitive edge

promotes quality awareness

emphasizes quality enhancement

provides total quality assurance

is fully committed to quality assurance

demonstrates accuracy, thoroughness and orderliness in performing work assignments

performs with unusual accuracy, thoroughness and effectiveness

shows professional concern for quality work

encourages all employees to be alert for defects

excels in detecting flaws or imperfections

quality of work is consistently high

achieves the highest standard of excellence

is committed to excellence

strives for state-of-the-art perfection

displays pride in work

RESOURCEFULNESS

demonstrates self-reliance and resourcefulness

is extremely resourceful and enthusiastic

draws on strong personal resources when faced with difficult situations

capitalizes on personal strengths

maximizes individual resources and energies

optimizes the use of all available resources

makes effective use of all organizational resources

maximizes the use of organizational resources

makes optimum use of department resources

excels in resource utilization

is able to capitalize on hidden resources

allocates resources wisely

effectively uses all information sources

is very effective in using the Internet as a powerful resource

makes effective use of information and resources available from industry associations

RESOURCEFULNESS

develops resourceful solutions

achieves success when confronted with limited resources

effectively organizes, assembles and arranges resources to meet goals

effectively matches goals to resources

effectively matches resources with objectives

effectively assesses employee resources, strengths and competencies

makes reasonable requests for additional resources and assistance

RESPONSIBILITY

devotes appropriate attention to all responsibilities

accepts responsibility for own decisions and those of subordinates

assumes responsibility for mistakes and shortcomings of subordinates

takes total responsibility for actions of subordinates

accepts full responsibility for results

is willing to accept ultimate responsibility

honors all commitments

accepts responsibility for compliance with rules and regulations

continues to seek and accept responsibility

seizes responsibility

takes positive action to meet growing responsibility

delegates responsibility effectively

is especially effective in assigning responsibility

builds personal accountability

displays a willingness to face conflicts

accepts new job assignments willingly

eagerly seeks formidable challenges

is eager to accept challenging assignments

views new assignments as an opportunity for growth

establishes policies reflecting strong support of corporate responsibility

SALES MANAGEMENT

consistently meets sales objectives by (__) percent

excels in managing geographically dispersed sales operations

responds quickly to changing market conditions

keeps alert to new marketing opportunities

excels in developing new markets

continuously explores new markets

keeps alert to all sales opportunities

keeps alert to new products

makes a strong contribution to pricing policies and strategies

keeps pricing strategies consistent with profitability goals

hires individuals with a high probability of selling success

excels in recruiting and retaining talented sales personnel

is able to retain high performance representatives

SALES MANAGEMENT

provides strong sales incentives

makes effective use of sales meetings to motivate and train

recognizes the value of sales training

makes effective use of marketing research

gives appropriate attention to large accounts

is skillful in obtaining high level appointments

demonstrates a strong ability to prevent large customers from switching to competitors

gives sufficient attention to smaller accounts to increase potential

gives appropriate attention to all distribution channels

is very successful in developing sales through distributors

excels in developing distributor loyalty

is very successful in building incremental sales

impresses on the entire organization the need to treat customers courteously and fairly

keeps abreast of the latest trends in Internet selling

SELLING SKILLS

achieves continuous sales growth

is a top sales producer

is a top sales performer

is a solid sales producer

is a sales leader

develops sound call frequency patterns

follows effective call frequency patterns

maintains an excellent sales to call ratio

is very creative in generating leads

follows-up on all leads

is very effective in turning leads into sales

excels in obtaining new customers

is comfortable in making cold calls

turns prospects into well satisfied customers

displays strong selling skills

demonstrates persuasive selling skills

is skilled in arousing customer interest

SELLING SKILLS

uses effective sales approaches

displays a strong knowledge of product lines

capitalizes on all product features

excels in selling benefits

places emphasis on customer benefits

focuses on benefits

makes effective use of selling aids

makes effective use of advertising and promotion

is making effective use of technology to improve sales performance

makes effective use of testimonials

is very skilled in overcoming objections

excels in sales closing

follows sound pricing strategies

sells on the basis of value rather than price

is proficient in overcoming price resistance

is able to successfully overcome sales resistance

(continued)

SELLING SKILLS

recognizes the hidden motivations of customers

excels in uncovering real buying motives

effectively maintains control of sales situations

maintains a high degree of selling ethics

makes well prepared sales presentations

uses service as a powerful selling aid

emphasizes service to overcome price objections

recognizes the value of extraordinary services

provides exceptional customer service

impresses customers with excellent service

sells the value of service

recognizes the vital role of customer service

provides responsive follow-up service

excels in handling customer inquiries

excels in establishing customer credibility

makes customers feel satisfied and appreciated

continuously strives to improve customer satisfaction

is strong in developing customer satisfaction

concentrates on increasing customer satisfaction

keeps customers satisfied

gains the trust of customers

is highly regarded and trusted by accounts

builds customer loyalty

places a high priority on retaining customers

excels in customer retention

excels in developing repeat customers

maintains continuous customer contact

keeps customers first

excels in building long-term relationships with customers

continuously meets customer requirements

continuously meets customer expectations

excels in reactivating inactive accounts

(continued)

SELLING SKILLS

displays a strong knowledge of customer's business

focuses on customer needs

understands customer needs and wants

responds quickly to customer needs

displays a high level of empathy in customer relations

is responsive to changing customer demands

is very effective in training customer sales personnel

gains the full promotional support of marketers

effectively enforces company policies without alienating customers

promptly handles customer complaints and problems

handles customer complaints with tact and diplomacy

responds rapidly to customer feedback

uses complaints to provide valuable customer feedback

resolves customer problems at early stages

SELLING SKILLS

excels in solving customer problems

skillfully handles unreasonable requests and demands from customers

is skilled in refusing customer requests while presenting alternative solutions

is able to solve problems without having customers contact management

capitalizes on competitive advantages

handles competitive situations with confidence and tact

keeps well informed of the strengths and weaknesses of competitors

makes effective use of competitive analysis

makes effective use of company strengths to counter competitive offers

is very cooperative in sharing information with other sales personnel

is a strong contributor in team selling

is a strong participant in team selling

STRESS

successfully copes with demands from superiors, subordinates and peers

successfully handles multiple demands from superiors and subordinates

effectively copes with the stress of demanding duties

meets ever changing demands

performs effectively despite sudden deadlines and changing priorities

works effectively for multiple superiors

thrives on stressful situations

copes effectively with pressures and tensions

copes effectively with anxiety

copes effectively with adversity

effectively handles stress and anxiety

handles emergencies with coolness

is able to stay focused when faced with emergency situations

stays focused under turbulent conditions

demonstrates coolness under stress

maintains coolness despite annoyances

shows a strong resistance to annoyances

shows finesse in situations of stress

performs well in crisis situations

performs well under pressure

works effectively in high pressure situations

works calmly in a turbulent environment

is able to capably adjust to ever changing work environments

effectively copes with staff reductions

remains calm and professional when faced with tight deadlines

remains calm in crisis situations

remains powerful and effective while under stress

capably handles authority when confronted

keeps calm and professional under the toughest circumstances

handles unusual dilemmas with calmness

(continued)

STRESS

displays a calm demeanor

remains calm under pressure

remains calm in emotionally charged situations

remains courteous under pressure

gets things done calmly

displays impressive poise under stress

maintains poise in the toughest situations

shows poise when under pressure

maintains personal composure in high stress situations

handles crises with composure

projects composure

copes effectively with risk and uncertainty

adjusts promptly and calmly to change

handles the unexpected with coolness

successfully copes with unintended consequences

plans to deal effectively with anticipated stressful situations effectively manages stress

capably handles potentially volatile situations

makes strong mental preparations for stressful situations

makes positive use of stress to improve performance

makes effective use of humor to ease tensions

maintains control in all situations

is not controlled by events and crisis situations

remains in solid control

keeps stress under control

gains control over job pressures

recognizes stress-related problems

recognizes the impact of stress and burnout on organizational effectiveness

knows when to seek help

recognizes the importance of sound physical and mental health for top performance

SUPERVISORY SKILLS

excels in the supervision and leadership of subordinates

is a highly respected supervisor

excels in getting work done by others

makes certain that employees have a clear understanding of their responsibilities

develops precise job expectations

establishes realistic work demands

ensures cost-efficient assignment of employees

divides work into manageable activities

effectively schedules personnel for peak and slack periods

effectively balances work flow

effectively prevents over-staffing

gains maximum productivity from employees

optimizes productivity

makes maximum use of personnel and equipment

excels in equipment utilization

maximizes the performance of people and equipment

excels in preventing machinery breakdowns

maintains consistency of operations

takes prompt action to minimize down time

quickly eliminates trouble spots

strives to make more meaningful and challenging contributions to the betterment of the department

effectively motivates subordinates to exert the effort necessary to attain organizational goals

maintains a work situation which stimulates the growth of individuals

uses job enrichment to improve productivity

expects and demands superior performance

places emphasis on results

brings out the best in employees

gives constant encouragement to subordinates

gives constructive suggestions to subordinates

takes effective measures to eliminate job plateauing

(continued)

SUPERVISORY SKILLS

keeps employees challenged through job enrichment

challenges the abilities of subordinates

recognizes the important relationships between rewards, reinforcement and results

maximizes the value of recognition and rewards

makes effective use of constructive compliments

gives proper recognition

excels in giving verbal praise

develops a climate providing motivation, participation and opportunities for employee initiative

promotes an effective climate

encourages a climate for action

develops a productive work environment

promotes a comfortable, friendly organizational atmosphere

is readily accessible to subordinates

excels in encouraging employee involvement

encourages active involvement of staff

receives full support from staff

promotes positive involvement

stimulates individual participation

stimulates productive discussion sessions for positive action

effectively seeks and obtains ideas

properly asserts ideas

properly asserts authority

effectively communicates organizational policies and other information to subordinates

is effective in giving orders and directions

gives clear instructions

avoids over-supervising

hires qualified people

is strong in hiring resourceful and talented employees

effectively utilizes experienced employees to train new hires

(continued)

SUPERVISORY
SKILLS

effectively supervises temporary employees

makes effective use of temporary employees
to meet immediate needs

capably supervises former peers

capably supervises employees with more
experience

gives sound, practical advice

gains employee confidence

shows concern for the employee as a person

develops strong credibility with subordinates

understands different personalities and traits

capably manages diverse personalities

shows empathy

is sensitive to the feelings of others

shows genuine respect

shows warmth and consideration

supervises firmly and fairly

is fair and firm when dealing with subordinates

establishes acceptable tolerance levels

effectively handles employee problems and discontent

handles employee problems professionally

recognizes and deals with signs of employee unrest

encourages constructive feedback

responds quickly to feedback

turns complaints into opportunities

knows when to reprimand

knows when to ignore

knows when to confront

maintains order and discipline

effectively handles negative behavior

promptly disciplines inappropriate behavior

handles disruptive behavior with firmness

disciplines without compromising authority

disciplines without causing resentment

(continued)

SUPERVISORY SKILLS

uses positive techniques to discipline

uses constructive discipline

quickly settles disciplinary problems

promptly handles behavior problems before they become irreversible

takes prompt measures to prevent performance and behavior problems before becoming irreversible

keeps small situations from becoming big problems

takes prompt corrective action

handles problems immediately

corrects without criticizing

takes appropriate remedial action

quickly dispels unfounded rumors

settles disputes firmly

resolves conflicts constructively

is skilled in conflict resolution

closely monitors absenteeism and tardiness

gives appropriate attention to reducing absenteeism, tardiness and turnover

effectively controls employee absenteeism and
tardiness

strictly and uniformly enforces attendance
rules

decisively handles chronic absenteeism

overcomes personality conflicts

prevents personnel conflicts from reducing
productivity

capably manages the marginal performer

excels in revitalizing employees who are
coasting

capably handles difficult people

is skillful in supervising difficult people

capably handles resistance from staff
members

deals effectively with resistance

effectively deals with mistakes and errors

takes positive steps to avoid recurrence of
errors

(continued)

SUPERVISORY
SKILLS

copes effectively with misunderstandings

keeps well informed of new legislation affecting the workplace

maintains strict compliance with employment laws

keeps well informed of supervisory legal responsibilities

is able to take disciplinary action while conforming to all legal aspects

applies all rules and regulations fairly

promptly reports all incidents

prepares solid documentation before disciplining problem workers

ensures that all personnel problems are properly documented

promptly and thoroughly documents employee disciplinary action

closely follows all operating procedures

TACT AND DIPLOMACY

handles situations in a calm, objective manner

handles complaints with tact

is very confident in handling awkward situations

handles sensitive situations with confidence

accomplishes results without creating friction

avoids arguments

handles confrontations constructively

is very tactful when facing confrontation

refuses requests with tact and diplomacy

is tactful in conflict situations

makes tactful and appropriate responses

is cordial, tactful and firm

displays trust and mutual understanding

employs procedures that reveal poise

accepts constructive criticism

tactfully admits mistakes and errors

is tactful in correcting the mistakes of others

(continued)

157

TACT AND DIPLOMACY

is very polished in matters of etiquette

demonstrates polished etiquette skills

displays proper etiquette

handles visitors with grace and tact

excels in welcoming new employees

displays grace and style

follows proper protocol

is polite in all situations

displays excellent mannerisms

conveys sincere appreciation at every opportunity

TEAM SKILLS

develops an organizational culture that fosters teamwork

excels in building teams for success

excels in developing self-managed teams

excels in appointing people with complimentary skills for maximum team effort

capitalizes on the talents of all team members

encourages the full participation of all team members

makes effective use of team resources

expects all team members to make maximum contributions

makes maximum use of the diverse talents of team members

effectively draws on the strengths of all team members

excels in appointing interdisciplinary team members

builds strong teams to meet performance goals

is a strong team builder

(continued)

TEAM SKILLS

uses the synergistic power of team planning to achieve goals

uses the synergistic power of teamwork to achieve results

makes a valuable contribution to team objectives

excels in task-oriented team development

excels in developing harmony and greater productivity

successfully implements self-directed teams

resolves team conflicts with finesse

excels in developing team momentum, enthusiasm and pride

TECHNICAL SKILLS

develops strong camaraderie among technical team members

strives for maximum technical team performance

recognizes the many benefits of spirited technical teamwork

recognizes the value of technical team dynamics

builds a strong sense of technical teamwork and purpose

effectively blends management skills with technical expertise

excels in technology management

demonstrates a high level of technical competence

makes effective use of tecnological advances

keeps abreast of emerging technologies

keeps informed of new technologies in office automation

displays a thorough understanding of computer technology

(continued)

TECHNICAL SKILLS

incorporates the newest computer technologies

excels in using information technology to reduce costs

overcomes resistance to technological change

demonstrates strong technical knowledge

possesses highly specialized technical skills

understands sophisticated technical specifications

is able to write technical information in easily understood terms

uses the latest techniques to gain the competitive edge

makes effective use of technical support

TIME MANAGEMENT

achieves maximum time effectiveness

places a high value on time effectiveness

demonstrates effective allocation of time resources

identifies and eliminates time wasters

avoids becoming involved in endless details

avoids time snares

uses systematic methods to accomplish more in less time

delegates for maximum time effectiveness

sets realistic time goals

consistently meets all deadlines

makes effective use of peak time periods

maximizes peak times

uses time productively

uses time wisely

makes effective use of supervisors' time and resources

respects the time of others

(continued)

TIME MANAGEMENT

prepares meeting agendas that are concise and time saving

maintains strict time allotments for meetings

keeps meetings on schedule

makes effective use of travel time

works smarter, not harder

makes effective use of discretionary time

avoids confusing activity with accomplishment

VERSATILITY

possesses many talents and capabilities

possesses an unique combination of skills

demonstrates competence in many areas

has the ability to perform a wide range of
assignments

performs a broad range of assignments with
efficiency and accuracy

effectively handles concurrent assignments

successfully handles multiple projects at the
same time

is very capable of handling a multitude of
situations

displays versatile expertise

demonstrates diversified skills

extremely versatile

effectively handles special assignments

displays flexibility in adapting to changing
conditions

effectively copes with accelerating changes

is flexible and open toward change

(continued)

VERSATILITY

is receptive to change

is successfully demonstrating the ability to develop from a specialist to a generalist

is capable of maintaining essential operations covering a variety of functions

extremely valuable in providing back-up support for other jobs

is able to provide broad organizational support in many areas

VISION

recognizes the importance of strategic planning, mission and vision statements

promotes strong support of mission and vision statements

keeps employees informed of mission statements and purposes

conveys a clear understanding of the organization's mission

develops vision statements that reflect realistic solutions

promotes broad support of management visions

excels in communicating the organization's philosophy

is very effective in creating shared vision

displays visionary leadership skills

is a visionary leader

displays multi-faceted vision

displays long-term vision

excels in visionary thinking

is a visionary thinker

(continued)

VISION

displays a clear vision of goals

formulates effective plans and envisions goals

is able to turn visions into actual action plans

is a visionary planner

demonstrates an ability to transfer vision into realities

develops strategic vision

excels in visionary strategies

inspires visions of future successes

WRITING ABILITY

writes letters, memos and reports that command attention and achieve results

effectively and efficiently handles correspondence

makes effective use of electronic writing

writes with remarkable clarity and consistency

writes precisely and effectively

demonstrates creative writing ability

writes to convey a positive impression

writes in a positive tone

writes in a positive manner to reflect favorably upon the organization

writes reports that achieve maximum impact

is a persuasive writer

writes proposals that win approval

prepares concise and meaningful reports

writes to ensure readability

ensures that correspondence is reader friendly

(continued)

WRITING ABILITY

excels in converting complex information into simple, readable form

is skilled in using technical terminology

is very proficient in writing manuals, policies and procedures

is highly skilled in preparing reports and proposals

is very skillful in writing on controversial subjects

places emphasis on meaningful action words

demonstrates strong grammar and usage skills

displays strong skills in using correct grammar and punctuation

possesses a large vocabulary

excels in rewriting, editing and proofreading

demonstrates strong proofreading skills

is a highly competent proofreader

demonstrates strong editing skills

II. TWO WORD PHRASES

TWO WORD PHRASES

accelerating changes
accepting responsibility
accomplishing results
accumulated knowledge
accurate assessments
accurate documentation
achievement-oriented
achieving excellence
achieving results
action-oriented
action plans
active participant
administrative efficiency
administrative strategies
administrative support
alternative solutions
analytical framework
analytical methods
analytical qualities
analytical reasoning
analytical techniques
analytical thinking
anticipated performance
anticipating needs
appropriate measures
audit controls
available resources
basic strengths

(continued)

TWO WORD PHRASES

broad perspective
broadest discretion
career building
career development
challenging opportunities
challenging problems
changing assignments
changing conditions
changing priorities
changing situations
clear expectations
communication skills
competent communicator
competent performer
competing priorities
competitive advantage
competitive edge
computer application
computer generated
computer technologies
concentrated effort
concurrent assignments
confident speaker
consensus-builder
considerable flexibility
consistently high
constructive actions
constructive criticism

TWO WORD PHRASES

constructive feedback

constructive ideas

contemporary management

contingency plans

continuing confidence

continuing efforts

continuous improvement

controlling expenses

conveying professionalism

core competencies

core components

core principles

core strengths

core values

corrective actions

corrective measures

cost conscious

cost control

cost effectiveness

cost implications

cost priorities

cost reductions

creative alternatives

creative excellence

creative solutions

creative strategies

creative strengths

creative support

(continued)

TWO WORD PHRASES

crisis situations
critical challenges
critical elements
critical factors
critical incidents
critical role
critical skills
critical solutions
critical thinker
customer demands
customer needs
customer-oriented
customer satisfaction
damage control
decisive action
delegating solutions
desired results
developing solutions
distinguishing characteristics
diversified approaches
diversified skills
driving force
dynamic impressions
effective marketing
effective presentations
effective systems
efficient manner
eliminating waste

TWO WORD PHRASES

emerging technologies
emerging trends
eminently qualified
energy drive
enthusiastic spirit
essential knowledge
essential skills
exceeds expectations
exceptional progress
exciting challenges
expected production
extra efforts
extremely industrious
extremely resourceful
favorable impression
first impressions
formidable challenges
fresh enthusiasm
fresh ideas
fresh insights
fresh perspective
fresh thinking
fullest support
fully documented
fully prepared
future-oriented
genuine interest
global thinking

(continued)

TWO WORD PHRASES

goal achiever
goal attainment
goal seeker
greater achievement
greater contribution
greatest return
growth potential
hands-on
hidden strengths
hidden talents
high achiever
high output
high payoff
high potential
high profile
high quality
highest priority
highly articulate
highly committed
highly competent
highly dependable
highly energized
highly regarded
highly sophisticated
highly supportive
ignites enthusiasm
imaginative thinking
implementing change

TWO WORD PHRASES

important contributor

impressive results

improving quality

improving techniques

increasing efficiency

independent decisions

individual strengths

individual values

information sources

initiating solutions

inner drive

innovative developments

innovative insight

innovative planning

innovative possibilities

innovative solutions

innovative thinking

innovative trends

inspiring subordinates

intense desire

job enlargement

job enrichment

job plateauing

keen interest

key characteristics

key element

leadership qualities

leadership role

(continued)

TWO WORD PHRASES

learning experience
learning opportunities
logical sequence
logical thinking
loyal support
maintaining control
maintaining momentum
major contributor
management effectiveness
management efficiency
management expectations
management principles
management support
maximizing resources
maximum effectiveness
maximum efficiency
maximum effort
maximum impact
maximum productivity
maximum results
maximum return
measurable results
meeting deadlines
mental toughness
meticulous attention
moral soundness
most respected
multi-faceted

TWO WORD PHRASES

multi-task

multiple demands

multiple resources

multiple skills

multiple superiors

mutual benefit

mutual gain

mutual success

negotiating skills

new approaches

new concepts

new customers

new perspectives

new strategies

new technologies

newly created

open communications

open-minded

operating knowledge

operating skills

opinion leader

optical outcomes

optimal results

optimal targets

optimum advantage

optimum productivity

optional solutions

organizational effectiveness

(continued)

TWO WORD PHRASES

organizational expectations
organizational goals
organizational resources
organizational support
peak efficiency
peak performance
peak times
performance conscious
performance levels
performance measurement
performance targets
personal accountability
personal commitment
personal effectiveness
personal impact
personal integrity
personal magnetism
personal strengths
personal traits
personal values
personal visibility
persuasive ability
planning approaches
planning decisions
planning solutions
planning techniques
pleasing personality
positive attitude

TWO WORD PHRASES

positive attributes
positive direction
positive expectations
positive force
positive image
positive impact
positive reinforcement
powerful commitment
practical applications
practical insights
practical skills
practical solutions
practical thinking
presentation skills
prime mover
priority determinations
problem solving
productive cooperation
productive impact
professional competence
professional development
professional effectiveness
professional ethics
professional excellence
professional expertise
professional horizons
professional participation
professional skills

(continued)

TWO WORD PHRASES

professional trends
profit-conscious
profit-minded
profit-oriented
promoting teamwork
prompt measures
proper perspective
proven performer
proven techniques
quality enhancement
reader friendly
realistic objectives
realistic solutions
realistically enthusiastic
renewed energy
resource application
resource utilization
resourceful solutions
results focused
results-oriented
risk-taking
root causes
safety conscious
sales opportunities
sales producer
satisfying solutions
secretarial support
self-development

TWO WORD PHRASES

self-directed
self-discipline
self-pacing
self-starter
selling skills
sensitive situations
shared drive
shared values
shared vision
significant contribution
simplified solutions
simplified systems
skill development
smooth transition
solid achiever
solid background
solid contributor
solid direction
solid experience
solid foundation
solid reputation
solid skills
solid techniques
solid understanding
solution seeker
sound conclusions
sound controls
sound decisions

(continued)

TWO WORD PHRASES

special assignments
specialized skills
speech proficiency
stimulating action
strategic aims
strategic alternatives
strategic design
strategic opportunities
strategic plans
strategic thrust
strategic vision
strategically-oriented
strategicaly positioned
strategically sound
stress tolerance
stressful solutions
strong contributor
strong effort
strong impact
strong performer
strong perseverance
strong potential
strongly qualified
substantial contribution
success-oriented
support applications
support services
supportive relationships

TWO WORD PHRASES

supportive skills
sustained commitment
sustained energy
sustained performance
synergistic benefit
systematic approach
systematic results
team effort
team motivator
team performance
team spirit
technical competence
thinks futuristically
time-efficient
top performer
total involvement
tracking progress
training needs
trouble shooting
ultimate responsibility
unique approaches
unique combination
unique expertise
unique insights
unique methods
unique problems
unique talents
unique value

(continued)

TWO WORD PHRASES

user-friendly
valuable insight
verbal commitments
visionary leadership
visionary strategies
well-informed
working knowledge
works effectively
world-class
zero tolerances

III. HELPFUL ADJECTIVES

HELPFUL ADJECTIVES

absolute
abundant
accurate
active
adaptable
adept
affirmative
alert
ambitious
analytical
articulate
authoritave
calm
capable
challenging
charismatic
clear-thinking
cohesive
compelling
competent
complete
composed
comprehensive
concise
confident

conscientious
considerable
consistent
constructive
cooperative
courageous
courteous
creative
curious
decisive
dedicated
definite
dependable
desirable
determined
diligent
diplomatic
discreet
distinctive
dynamic
eager
effective
efficient
eminent
energetic

(continued)

HELPFUL ADJECTIVES

enlightening

enterprising

enthusiastic

excellent

exceptional

exciting

extra

extraordinary

extreme

factual

fair

favorable

fine

flawless

flexible

forceful

foremost

formidable

forward-looking

frank

genuine

good-natured

great

hands-on

harmonious

helpful

high

high-tech

honest

imaginative

immense

impeccable

important

independent

industrious

informative

ingenious

innovative

instrumental

intense

interactive

inventive

invigorating

involved

keen

knowledgeable

lasting

latent

latest

logical

HELPFUL ADJECTIVES

loyal

magnificent

major

mature

maximum

meaningful

meticulous

motivated

neat

objective

observant

open-minded

opportunistic

optimal

optimistic

orderly

organized

original

outstanding

patient

perceptive

perfect

persevering

persuasive

pleasant

poised

polished

positive

powerful

practical

precise

predictable

preeminent

premier

proactive

productive

professional

profound

progressive

prolific

prominent

proper

prudent

punctual

quick

rational

realistic

reliable

remarkable

resourceful

(continued)

HELPFUL ADJECTIVES

respectful
responsive
rigorous
self-confident
self-demanding
significant
sincere
sizable
sophisticated
sound
special
splendid
state-of-the-art
steadfast
stellar
stern
stimulating
stringent
strong
successful
superb
superior

supportive
synergistic
systematic
tactful
tedious
thorough
trustworthy
truthful
ultimate
understanding
unique
unlimited
unusual
utmost
valuable
versatile
vibrant
vigorous
well-liked
winning
worthy
zestful

IV. HELPFUL VERBS

HELPFUL VERBS

accelerates
accentuates
accepts
accomplishes
accounts
achieves
acquaints
acquires
activates
acts
actuates
adapts
addresses
adheres
adjusts
administers
adopts
advances
advises
allocates
amplifies
analyzes
anticipates
applies
appoints

appraises
appropriates
approves
arises
arranges
articulates
ascends
ascertains
aspires
assembles
asserts
assesses
assigns
assimilates
assists
assumes
assures
attains
attempts
attends
audits
augments
authorizes
averts
avoids

(continued)

HELPFUL VERBS

broadens

builds

calculates

capitalizes

captivates

centralizes

challenges

checks

circulates

clarifies

clears

coaches

collaborates

collects

combines

commands

communicates

compels

compiles

completes

complies

composes

comprehends

computes

conceives

concentrates

concludes

condenses

conducts

conforms

conjects

considers

consolidates

consults

consummates

contemplates

continues

contributes

controls

converts

conveys

cooperates

coordinates

copes

corrects

creates

cultivates

decentralizes

decreases

dedicates

HELPFUL VERBS

defines
delegates
delivers
demonstrates
deploys
deserves
designates
designs
determines
develops
devises
devotes
directs
discharges
discovers
discusses
displays
disseminates
distinguishes
distributes
documents
drafts
earns
edits
educates

effects
elicits
eliminates
emanates
embellishes
embraces
emphasizes
employs
empowers
emulates
enables
encompasses
encourages
energizes
enforces
engenders
enhances
enlightens
enriches
ensures
envisions
establishes
estimates
evaluates
evidences

(continued)

199

HELPFUL VERBS

evokes

examines

exceeds

excels

executes

exemplifies

exercises

exhibits

expands

expects

expedites

explores

expresses

extends

extracts

faces

facilitates

focuses

follows-up

forecasts

foresees

forms

formulates

fosters

fulfills

furnishes

gains

generates

gives

grasps

guides

handles

helps

identifies

impacts

implements

impresses

improves

improvises

increases

influences

informs

initiates

inspects

inspires

installs

instills

institutes

instructs

insures

HELPFUL VERBS

integrates

interacts

interprets

interviews

introduces

invents

investigates

invests

invokes

issues

judges

keeps

knows

launches

leads

learns

lectures

maintains

makes

manages

markets

maximizes

mediates

meets

minimizes

mobilizes

modifies

monitors

motivates

necessitates

negotiates

neutralizes

notifies

observes

obtains

operates

optimizes

orchestrates

orders

organizes

originates

overcomes

oversees

paces

participates

perceives

performs

perpetuates

plans

possesses

(continued)

HELPFUL VERBS

practices

prepares

presents

presumes

prevents

prioritizes

processes

procures

produces

programs

projects

promotes

proposes

protects

provides

pursues

radiates

realizes

receives

recognizes

recommends

reconciles

records

recruits

reduces

refines

reflects

regards

regulates

reinforces

rejects

relates

releases

relies

reports

represents

requires

researches

resolves

resonates

respects

responds

restores

retains

reviews

revises

revitalizes

schedules

secures

seeks

HELPFUL VERBS

sells

serves

settles

shows

simplifies

solves

sorts

sparks

specifies

stimulates

strengthens

strives

structures

studies

submits

suggests

supervises

supports

surmounts

surpasses

surveys

sustains

takes

targets

thinks

tolerates

trains

transacts

translates

treats

uncovers

understands

undertakes

unifies

uses

utilizes

verifies

vitalizes

weighs

widens

works

writes

V. PERFORMANCE RANKINGS

PERFORMANCE RANKINGS

exceptional

superior

extraordinary

fair

excellent

satisfactory

distinguished

substandard

outstanding

unsatisfactory

very good

unacceptable

good

VI. TIME FREQUENCY

TIME FREQUENCY

always

usually

frequently

often

continuously

sometimes

occasionally

rarely

seldom

never

VII. GUIDELINES FOR SUCCESSFUL EVALUATIONS

GUIDELINES FOR SUCCESSFUL EVALUATIONS

I. RATE OBJECTIVELY

You can improve the accuracy of your ratings by recognizing the following factors that subvert evaluations:

1. THE HALO EFFECT:

The tendency of an evaluator to rate a person good or bad on all characteristics based on an experience or knowledge involving only one dimension.

2. LENIENCY TENDENCY:

A tendency toward evaluating all persons as outstanding and to give inflated ratings rather than true assessments of performance.

3. STRICTNESS TENDENCY:

The opposite of the leniency tendency; that is, a bias toward rating all persons at the low end of the scale and a tendency to be overly demanding or critical.

4. AVERAGE TENDENCY:

A tendency to evaluate every person as average regardless of major differences in performance.

(continued)

Legislation, court cases and government directives have added a new dimension to the performance appraisal process. Employee evaluations may become a key issue in litigation. Clearly, the accuracy of performance appraisals is a requirement of the highest priority.

II. USE SIGNIFICANT DOCUMENTATION AND FACTUAL EXAMPLES

It is essential that performance evaluations be measured in relation to any pre-existing standards, objectives or other specific job requirements.

Most appraisal systems require the rater to cite examples of performance. Examples should be objective and specific rather than subjective and general.

Whenever possible, use quantitative examples which can be expressed in numerical terms using figures, percentages or amounts. For example, it is preferable to state "exceeded sales objective by 10% through the first six months" rather than "exceeded sales objective."

II. PLAN FOR APPRAISAL INTERVIEW

The appraisal interview is one of the most important elements of the evaluation process. The purpose of the interview is to review performance and let people know how they are doing. You can improve the effectiveness of the interview by adhering to the following guidelines:

Select a quiet, comfortable and appropriate location

Plan to avoid interruptions

Allow ample time for the discussion

Put the person at ease

Conduct the interview in a positive manner

Review the ratings by category

Keep the interview performance-oriented

Encourage the person to talk, but remain firmly in control

Listen carefully

Avoid the defensive

Focus on patterns rather than isolated instances

(continued)

respond to objections, problems and disagreements

concentrate on facts

be honest

be a coach, not a judge

place emphasis on positive reinforcement

develop positive action plans

end the interview on a positive and supportive basis

V. EMPHASIZE FUTURE DEVELOPMENT

Effective performance appraisal programs place emphasis on planning for future development. The attainment of organizational goals coupled with maximum employee growth is the mark of true management success. You can develop the full potential of subordinates by implementing the following:

1. Analyze performance and develop appropriate strategies for strengthening areas in need of improvement.

2. Develop a goal-oriented plan to prepare for greater responsibility.

3. Establish follow-up plans to ensure employee growth.

4. Use positive reinforcement to motivate.

V. EMPHASIZE THE POSITIVE

The positive use of performance appraisals combined with sound management practice will contribute to the improved effectiveness of every organization.

NOTES/COMMENTS

NOTES/COMMENTS

NOTES/COMMENTS

ISBN 1-882423-10-0

EAN

9 781882 423101

51095